REACTJS DEVELOPMENT

SANDEEP BISHT

REACTJS DEVELOPMENT

Contents

WHAT IS REACTJS AND DEVELOPMENT

React is a front-end library developed by Facebook. It is used for handling the view layer for web and mobile apps. ReactJS allows us to create reusable UI components. It is currently one of the most popular JavaScript libraries and has a strong foundation and large community behind it.

What is Reactjs used for and advantages ?

React. js is an open-source JavaScript library that is used for building user interfaces specifically for single-page applications. It's used for handling the view layer for web and mobile apps. React also allows us to create reusable UI components

ADVANTAGES

Intuitive

ReactJS is extremely intuitive to work with and provides interactivity to the layout of any UI. Plus, it enables fast and quality assured application development that in turn saves tome for both - clients and developers.

Declarative

ReactJS enables significant data changes that result in automatic alteration in the selected parts of user interfaces. Owing to this progressive functionality, there is no additional function that you need to perform to update your user interface.

Provides Reusable Components

ReactJS provides reusable components that developers have the authority to reuse and create a new application . Reusability is exactly like a remedy for developers. This platform gives the developers the authority to reuse the components build for some other application having the same functionality. Thereby, reducing the development effort and ensuring a flawless performance.

JavaScript library

A strong blend of JavaScript and HTML syntax is always used, which automatically simplifies the entire process of writing code for the planned project. The JS library consists several functions including one that converts the HTML components into required functions and transforms the entire project so that it is easy to understand.

Components Support

ReactJS is a perfect combination of JavaScript and HTML tags. The usage of the HTML tags and JS codes, make it easy to deal with a vast set of data containing the document object model. During this time, ReactJS works as a mediator which represents the DOM and assists to decide which component needs changes to get the exact results.

SEO-friendly

React JS was introduced after immense research and improvements by Facebook. Naturally, it stands out from the crowd and allows developers to build amazing, SEO-friendly user interfaces across browsers and engines.

Proficient Data Binding

ReactJS trails one-way data binding. This means that absolutely anyone can track all the changes made to any particular segment of the data. This is a symbol of its simplicity.

Why Use ReactJS For Application Development ?

Easy to Learn

React is an easy to learn and lightweight javascript library. Javascript developers can learn and start coding application in ReactJS with two three days of training.

Components Library

ReactJS is a component based technology. These components are the building blocks of development and can be shared and reused multiple times.

Developer Tools

React has two developer tools – React Developer Tools and Redux Developer Tools. These tools render a great help with application development.

React Native

React Native can be used to create native mobile apps for Android and iOS. React Native is a javascript library used for developing native applications.

Testability

React applications are easy to test. Different views of ReactJS application can be treated as functions of the state, which can then be manipulated to test output.

React is Declarative

With React you just need to describe the user interface. React then builds the actual user interface in the web browser.

LIMITATION OF REACTJS

React Technology accelerates so fast so that it cannot make proper documentation of the project. So, the developer tries to write the instruction on its own. React focus on the view part of MVC **i.e.** UI of the web application. Basically react allows developers to create large web applications that can change data, without reloading the page. The main purpose of React is to be fast, scalable, and simple. It works only on user interfaces in the application.

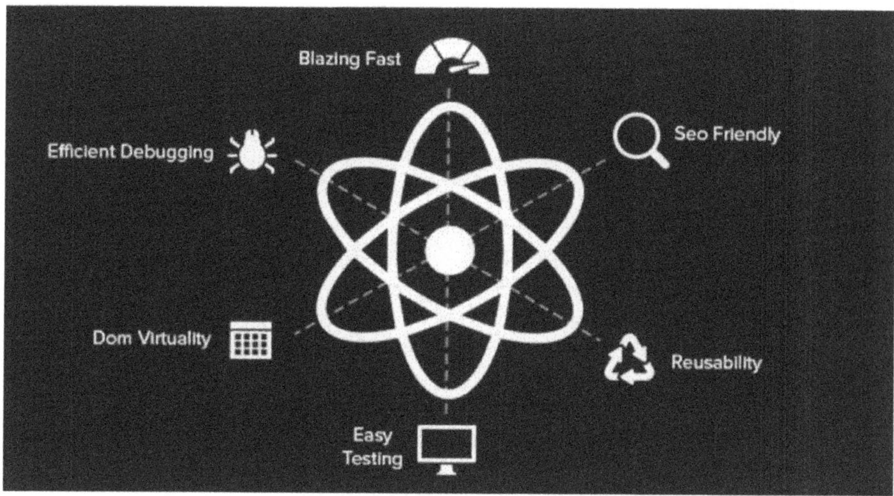

Why we choose Reactjs and why reactjs different from other libraries and framework like Angular.

Comparison Matrix	Angular	React
Purpose	Angular is quite helpful in detecting the execution errors at early stage. It is included with unit tests which aim to detect errors on their own.	React Library resolves only specific run-time errors since it has certain designed functions. Herein, developers can set up standards of quality and adequate processes to prevent the flaws in an application.
Performance	Angular is highly managed to combat against the React.js performance. It is based on "Dirty Checking" strategy to improve the negative impact on the performance.	One of the main hurdles with the React library is its performance. It always requires a copy of DOM in the memory to calculate the changes in the real DOM.
Language	TypeScript + RxJS as an additional feature to learn	JSX syntax for learning
Learning Curve	Angular is not simple due to its inherent complexity	Easy to understand framework and takes very less time to set up a single project.
Data Binding	It uses bi-directional data binding which is helpful in writing less code	It uses uni-directional data binding which connotes data flow in only one direction
Directives	Using directives in Angular is an effective way to work with DOM.	React Framework doesn't include any directives and hence all template logic should be written by itself.

Basis	AngularJS	ReactJS
Developer	Google	Facebook
Language	JavaScript	JSX
Type	JavaScript framework	Open-source JS library
Packaging	Weak	Strong
Data binding	Bi-directional	Uni-directional
Learning curve	High	Low
Toolchain	Low	High
DOM	DOM, Regular	Virtual DOM
App architecture	MVC	None

ENVIRONMENT SETUP

I will show you how to set up an environment for successful React development. For that there are some steps. First of all we will need NodeJS, so if you don't have it installed, check this link: **https://nodejs.org/en/download/**

Please download NodeJS first then install it on system. NodeJS is the platform needed for the ReactJS development.

After successfully installing NodeJS, we can start installing React using npm. You can install ReactJS in two ways:

- **Using webpack and babel.**
- **Using the create-react-app command.**

Installing ReactJS using webpack and babel

Webpack is a module bundler (manages and loads independent modules). It takes dependent modules and compiles them to a single (file) bundle. You can use this bundle while developing apps using command line or, by configuring it using webpack.config file.

Babel is a JavaScript compiler and transpiler. It is used to convert one source code to other. Using this you will be able to use the new ES6 features in your code where, babel converts it into plain old ES5 which can be run on all browsers.

Step 1 - Create the Root Folder

Create a folder with name reactApp on the desktop to install all the required files, using the mkdir command.

C:\Users\username\Desktop>mkdir reactApp

C:\Users\username\Desktop>cd reactApp

To create any module, it is required to generate the package.json file. Therefore, after Creating the folder, we need to create a package.json file. To do so you need to run the npm init command from the command prompt.

C:\Users\username\Desktop\reactApp>npm init

This command asks information about the module such as packagename, description, author etc. you can skip these using the –y option.

C:\Users\username\Desktop\reactApp>npm init -y

Wrote to C:\reactApp\package.json:

{ "name": "reactApp", "version": "1.0.0", "description": "", "main": "index.js", "scripts": { "test": "echo \"Error: no test specified\" && exit 1" }, "keywords": [], "author": "", "license": "ISC" }

<u>Step 2 - install React and react dom</u>

Since our main task is to install ReactJS, install it, and its dom packages, using install react and react-dom commands of npm respectively. You can add the packages we install, to package.json file using the --save option.

C:\Users\Tutorialspoint\Desktop\reactApp>npm install react --save
C:\Users\Tutorialspoint\Desktop\reactApp>npm install react-dom --save

Or, you can install all of them in single command as –

C:\Users\username\Desktop\reactApp>npm install react react-dom --save

<u>Step 3 - Install webpack</u>

Since we are using webpack to generate bundler install webpack, webpack-dev-server and webpack-cli.

C:\Users\username\Desktop\reactApp>npm install webpack --save C:\Users\username\Desktop\reactApp>npm install webpack-dev-server --save C:\Users\username\Desktop\reactApp>npm install webpack-cli --save

Or, you can install all of them in single command as –

C:\Users\username\Desktop\reactApp>npm install webpack webpack-dev-server webpack-cli --save

Step 4 - Install babel

Install babel, and its plugins babel-core, babel-loader, babel-preset-env, babel-preset-react and, html-webpack-plugin

C:\Users\username\Desktop\reactApp>npm install babel-core --save-dev C:\Users\username\Desktop\reactApp>npm install babel-loader --save-dev C:\Users\username\Desktop\reactApp>npm install babel-preset-env --save-dev C:\Users\username\Desktop\reactApp>npm install babel-preset-react --save-dev C:\Users\username\Desktop\reactApp>npm install html-webpack-plugin --save-dev

Or, you can install all of them in single command as –

C:\Users\username\Desktop\reactApp>npm install babel-core babel-loader babel-preset-env babel-preset-react html-webpack-plugin --save-dev

Step 5 - Create the Files

To complete the installation, we need to create certain files namely, index.html, App.js, main.js, webpack.config.js and, .babelrc. You can create these files manually or, using command prompt.

C:\Users\username\Desktop\reactApp>type nul > index.html C:\Users\username\Desktop\reactApp>type nul > App.js C:\Users\username\Desktop\reactApp>type nul > main.js C:\Users\username\Desktop\reactApp>type nul > webpack.config.js C:\Users\username\Desktop\reactApp>type nul > .babelrc

Step 6 - Set Compiler, Server and Loaders

Open webpack-config.js file and add the following code. We are setting webpack entry point to be main.js. Output path is the place where bundled app will be served. We are also setting the development server to 8001 port. You can choose any port you want.

webpack.config.js

```
const path = require('path');

const HtmlWebpackPlugin = require('html-webpack-plugin');

module.exports = { entry: './main.js',

output: { path: path.join(__dirname, '/bundle'),

filename: 'index_bundle.js' },

devServer: { inline: true, port: 8001 },

module: { rules: [ { test: /\.jsx?$/,

exclude: /node_modules/,

loader: 'babel-loader',

query: { presets: ['es2015', 'react']

}}

]

},

plugins:[ new HtmlWebpackPlugin({ template: './index.html' }) ] }
```

Open the package.json and delete "test" "echo \"Error: no test specified\" && exit 1" inside "scripts" object. We are deleting this line since we will not do any testing in this tutorial. Let's add the start and build commands instead.

"start": "webpack-dev-server --mode development --open --hot", "build": "webpack --mode production"

Step 7 - index.html

This is just regular HTML. We are setting div id = "app" as a root element for our app and adding index_bundle.js script, which is our bundled app file.

```
<!DOCTYPE html>

<html lang = "en">

<head>

<meta charset = "UTF-8">

<title>React App</title>

</head>

<body>

<div id = "app"></div>

<script src = 'index_bundle.js'></script>

</body>

</html>
```

I

Prototype & Prototype Inheritance

Inheritance: One object trying to access methods of other object.

Prototype: Prototypes are the mechanism by which JavaScript objects inherit features from one another.

Example:

```
let arr = ["Sandeep", "Bisht"];
let object ={
name: "Sandeep",
city:"Delhi",
getIntro: function(){
console.log(this.name + "from" + this.city);
}
}
```

When we create any javascript object. Javascript engine automatically without even let in you know attaches your object with some hidden properties and function. These are the hidden properties and function you can access it by using object dot(.) . It's not with the case of object if you create a function

Example:

```
function fun (){
//
}
```

and we check it will show the access of lots of things like call, apply, bind, argument, caller, etc. when we check in console. Whenever we create anything in javascript even a variable they get access to some of the hidden properties and methods. So these come wire prototype

Whenever we create any object javascript engine put this hidden properties into an object and attaches to our object.

arr_proto_.

This is the object where javascript engine putting all these functions and methods. If we add any dot (.) after object.

Prototype chain: Each object has a private property which holds a link to another object called its prototype. That prototype object has a prototype of its own, and so on until an object is reached with null as its prototype. By definition, null has no prototype, and acts as the final link in this prototype chain.

Example:

arr_proto_

Array.prototype

arr._proto_._proto_

Object.prototype

arr._proto_._proto_._proto_ null

Whenever we create an array it has it's prototype which is **arr_proto_** also have it's own chain.

Prototype Inheritance: The Prototypal Inheritance is a feature in javascript used to add methods and properties in objects. It is a method by which an object can inherit the properties and methods of another object.

II

High Order Functions & Components

A function which takes another function as an argument or return a function from it is known as higher order function.

Example:

think we have a function x. In it we also have a function y which takes x as an argument and calls x

```
function x() {
console.log("Sandeep");
}
function y(x) {
x();
}
```

Now see in this example this function y is taking another function x as an argument. Here x as an argument is higher order function.

X of above top is callback function. y is the higher order function.

Example:

```
const radius = [3, 1, 2, 4];
const calculateArea = function (radius) {
const output = [];
for(let i =0; i < radius.length; i++) {
output.push(Math.PI * radius[i] * radius[i]);
}
return output;
```

```
};
console.log(calculateArea (radius));
```

High Order Component: A higher-order component (HOC) is an advanced technique in React for reusing component logic. HOCs are not part of the React API, per se. They are a pattern that emerges from React's compositional nature. Concretely, a higher-order component is a function that takes a component and returns a new component.

One component that takes an another component as a props and returns an another component. That is HOC.

Simple component that takes component input and return a component input as an output.

Example:

```
import React, { useRef, useState } from "react"
function App() {
return (
<div className="App">
<h1> HOC </h1>
<HOCRed cmp={counter} />
<HOCGreen cmp={counter} />
</div>
);
}
function HOCRed(props)
{
return <h2 style={{backgroundColor: "red", width: "100"}}> <props. cmp /> </h2>
}
function HOCGreen(props)
{
return <h2 style={{backgroundColor: "green", width: "100"}}> <props. cmp /> </h2>
}
function Counter()
{
const [count, setCount]= useState(0)
return
<div>
<h3>{count} </h3>
```

```
<button onclick={()=>setCount(count+1)}> Update </button>
</div>
}
export default App;
```

III

Controlled & Uncontrolled Components

when we use ref, dom, anything in react code that time it is uncontrolled component.

```
import React, { Component } from 'react';
export default class App extends Component {
handleSubmit = () => {
console.log(this._name.value)
}
render() {
return (
<div>
<input type="text" ref={(input) => this._name = input} />
<button onclick={this.handleSubmit}> Submit</button>
</div>
```

Uncontroll any content in this input box that only in DOM not in a state. when a user type that time content is not accessable means during filling that input box and submit that time it will not remove that particular input box, content and submit button. Because it's not in state.

Controlled Component

Controlled components are those which is accessible and which is in state. Where the data is accessible from state.

Example:

```
this.setState({
name:event.target.value
})
}
handleSubmit = () => {
console.log(this._name.value)
}
render() {
return (
<div>
<input type="text" value={this.state.name} onChange={this.onInputChange} />
<button disabled={this.state.name.length ? false : true } onClick={this.handleSubmit}> Submit </ button>
</div>
```

If you see in this example the data is coming in value from state.

IV

Router

Install React Router

Install the react router using below command.

npm install react-router-dom --save

Concept

React router provides four components to manage navigation in React application.

Router – Router is th top level component. It encloses the entire application.

Link – Similar to anchor tag in html. It sets the target url along with reference text.

```
<Link to="/">Home</Link>
```

Switch & Route – Both are used together. Maps the target url to the component. Switch is the parent component and Route is the child component. Switch component can have multiple Route component and each Route component mapping a particular url to a component.

```
<Switch>
<Route exact path="/">
<Home />
</Route>
<Route path="/home">
<Home />
</Route>
<Route path="/list">
<ExpenseEntryItemList />
</Route>
```

```
</Switch>
```

Here, path attribute is used to match the url. Basically, Switch works similar to traditional switch statement in a programming language. It matches the target url with each child route (path attribute) one by one in sequence and invoke the first matched route.

Along with router component, React router provides option to get set and get dynamic information from the url. For example, in an article website, the url may have article type attached to it and the article type needs to be dynamically extracted and has to be used to fetch the specific type of articles.

```
<Link to="/article/c">C Programming</Link>
<Link to="/article/java">Java Programming</Link>
...
...
<Switch>
<Route path="article/:tag" children={<ArticleList />} />
</Switch>
```

Then, in the child component (class component),

```
import { withRouter } from "react-router"
class ArticleList extends React.Component {
...
...
static getDerivedStateFromProps(props, state) {
let newState = {
tag: props.match.params.tag
}
return newState;
}
...
...
}
export default WithRouter(ArticleList)
```

Here, **WithRouter** enables **ArticleList** component to access the tag information through props.

The same can be done differently in functional components –

```
function ArticleList() {
let { tag } = useParams();
return (
```

```
<div>
<h3>ID: {id}</h3>
</div>
);
}
```

Here, **useParams** is a custom React Hooks provided by React Router component.

Nested routing

React router supports nested routing as well. React router provides another React Hooks, **useRouteMatch()** to extract parent route information in nested routes.

```
function ArticleList() { // get the parent url and the matched path let { path, url } = useRouteMatch(); return ( <div> <h2>Articles</h2> <ul> <li> <Link to={`${url}/pointer`}>C with pointer</Link> </li> <li> <Link to={`${url}/basics`}>C basics</Link> </li> </ul>
```

Here, **useRouteMatch** returns the matched path and the target url. url can be used to create next level of links and path can be used to map next level of components / screens.

Creating navigation

Let us learn how to do routing by creating the possible routing in our expense manager application. The minimum screens of the application are given below –

Home screen – Landing or initial screen of the application

Expense list screen – Shows the expense items in a tabular format

Expense add screen – Add interface to add an expense item

First, create a new react application, react-router-app using Create React App or Rollup bundler by following instruction in Creating a React application chapter.

Next, open the application in your favorite editor.

Next, create src folder under the root directory of the application.

Next, create components folder under src folder.

Next, create a file, Home.js under src/components folder and start editing.

Next, import React library.

import React from 'react';

Next, import Link from React router library.

import { Link } from 'react-router-dom'

Next, create a class, Home and call constructor with props.

```
class Home extends React.Component {
constructor(props) {
super(props);
}
}
```

Next, add **render()** method and show the welcome message and links to add and list expense screen.

```
render() { return ( <div> <p>Welcome to the React tutorial</p> <p><Link to="/list">Click here</Link> to view expense list</p> <p><Link to="/add">Click here</Link> to add new expenses</p> </div> ) }
```

Finally, export the component.

```
export default Home;
```

The complete source code of the Home component is given below –

```
import React from ’react‘; import { Link } from ’react-router-dom’ class Home extends React.Component { constructor(props) { super(props); } render() { return ( <div> <p>Welcome to the React tutorial</p> <p><Link to="/list">Click here</Link> to view expense list</p> <p><Link to="/add">Click here</Link> to add new expenses</p> </div> ) } } export default Home;
```

Next, create ExpenseEntryItemList.js file under src/components folder and create ExpenseEntryItemList component.

```
import React from ’react‘; import { Link } from ’react-router-dom’ class ExpenseEntryItemList extends React.Component { constructor(props) { super(props); } render() { return ( <div> <h1>Expenses</h1> <p><Link to="/add">Click here</Link> to add new expenses</p> <div> Expense list </div> </div> ) } } export default ExpenseEntryItemList;
```

Next, create ExpenseEntryItemForm.js file under src/components folder and create ExpenseEntryItemForm component.

```
import React from ’react‘; import { Link } from ’react-router-dom’ class ExpenseEntryItemForm extends React.Component { constructor(props) { super(props); } render() { return ( <div> <h1>Add Expense item</h1> <p><Link to="/list">Click here</Link> to view new expense list</p> <div> Expense form </div> </div> ) } } export default ExpenseEntryItemForm;
```

Next, create a file, App.css under src/components folder and add generic css styles.

```
html { font-family: sans-serif; } a{ text-decoration: none; } p, li, a{ font-size: 14px; } nav ul { width: 100%; list-style-type: none; margin: 0; padding: 0; overflow: hidden; background-color: rgb(235,235,235); }
```

```
nav li { float: left; } nav li a { display: block; color: black; text-align: center; padding: 14px 16px; text-decoration: none; font-size: 16px; } nav li a:hover { background-color: rgb(187, 202, 211); }
```

Next, create a file, App.js under src/components folder and start editing. The purpose of the App component is to handle all the screen in one component. It will configure routing and enable navigation to all other components.

Next, import React library and other components.

```
import React from 'react'; import Home from './Home' import ExpenseEntryItemList from './ExpenseEntryItemList' import ExpenseEntryItemForm from './ExpenseEntryItemForm' import './App.css'
```

Next, import React router components.

```
import { BrowserRouter as Router, Link, Switch, Route } from 'react-router-dom'
```

Next, write the **render()** method and configure routing.

```
function App() { return ( <Router> <div> <nav> <ul> <li> <Link to="/">Home</Link> </li> <li> <Link to="/list">List Expenses</Link> </li> <li> <Link to="/add">Add Expense</Link> </li> </ul> </nav>
<Switch> <Route path="/list"> <ExpenseEntryItemList /> </Route> <Route path="/add"> <ExpenseEntryItemForm /> </Route> <Route path="/"> <Home /> </Route> </Switch> </div> </Router> ); }
```

Next, create a file, index.js under the src folder and use App component.

```
import React from 'react'; import ReactDOM from 'react-dom'; import App from './components/App'; ReactDOM.render( <React.StrictMode> <App /> </React.StrictMode>, document.getElementById('root') );
```

Finally, create a public folder under the root folder and create index.html file.

```
<!DOCTYPE html> <html lang="en"> <head> <meta charset="utf-8"> <title>React router app</title> </head> <body> <div id="root"></div> <script type="text/JavaScript" src="./index.js"></script> </body> </html>
```

Next, serve the application using npm command.

```
npm start
```

V

ReactJS - JSX

JSX is like using html with javascript in react.js. but that html part is JSX in React.js. We recommend using it with React to describe what the UI should look like. JSX may remind you of a template language, but it comes with the full power of JavaScript. JSX produces React "elements".

It is a JavaScript extension that allows us to describe React's object tree using a syntax that resembles that of an HTML template. It is just an XML-like extension that allows us to write JavaScript that looks like markup and have it returned from a component.

We can use the above JSX in our React code like this:

```
class JSXDemo extends React.Component { render() { return <h1>This is JSX</h1>; } } ReactDOM.render(<JSXDemo />, document.getElementById('root'));
```

Expressions

JSX supports expression in pure JavaScript syntax. Expression has to be enclosed inside the curly braces, { }. Expression can contain all variables available in the context, where the JSX is defined. Let us create simple JSX with expression.

Example:

```
<script type="text/babel"> var cTime = new Date().toTimeString(); ReactDOM.render( <div><p>The current time is {cTime}</p></div>, document.getElementById('react-app') ); </script>
```

Output:

Here, cTime used in the JSX using expression. The output of the above code is as follows,

The Current time is 21:19:56 GMT+0530(India Standard Time)

Functions

JSX supports user defined JavaScript function. Function usage is similar to expression. Let us create a simple function and use it inside JSX.

Example:

```
<script type="text/babel"> var cTime = new Date().toTimeString(); ReactDOM.render( <div><p>The current time is {cTime}</p></div>, document.getElementById('react-app') ); </script>
```

Output:

Here, getCurrentTime() is used get the current time and the output is similar as specified below –

The Current time is 21:19:56 GMT+0530(India Standard Time)

Attributes

JSX supports HTML like attributes. All HTML tags and its attributes are supported. Attributes has to be specified using camelCase convention (and it follows JavaScript DOM API) instead of normal HTML attribute name. For example, class attribute in HTML has to be defined as className. The following are few other examples –

htmlFor instead of for

tabIndex instead of tabindex

onClick instead of onclick

Example:

```
<style> .red { color: red } </style> <script type="text/babel"> function getCurrentTime() { return new Date().toTimeString(); } ReactDOM.render( <div> <p>The current time is <span className="red">{getCurrentTime()}</span></p> </div>, document.getElementById('react-app') ); </script>
```

Output

The output is as follows –

The Current time is 22:36:55 GMT+0530(India Standard Time)

Expression in attributes

JSX supports expression to be specified inside the attributes. In attributes, double quote should not be used along with expression. Either expression or string using double quote has to be used. The above example can be changed to use expression in attributes.

```
<style> .red { color: red } </style> <script type="text/babel"> function getCurrentTime() { return new Date().toTimeString(); } var class_name = "red"; ReactDOM.render( <div> <p>The current time is <span className={class_name}>{getCurrentTime()}</span></p> </div>,
```

document.getElementById('react-app')); </script>

VI

ReactJS - Component

A React component represents a small chunk of user interface in a webpage. The primary job of a React component is to render its user interface and update it whenever its internal state is changed. In addition to rendering the UI, it manages the events belongs to its user interface. To summarize, React component provides below functionalities.

* Initial rendering of the user interface.
* Management and handling of events.
* Updating the user interface whenever the internal state is changed.

React component accomplish these feature using three concepts –

* **Properties** – Enables the component to receive input.
* **Events** – Enable the component to manage DOM events and end-user interaction.
* **State** – Enable the component to stay stateful. Stateful component updates its UI with respect to its state.

Creating a React component

React library has two component types. The types are categorized based on the way it is being created.

Functional Components: Functional Component is a plain javascript function which accepts props as an argument and returns a React element.

Class Components: It requires us to extend from React.Component and create a render function which returns a React element. Uses ES6 class.

The core difference between function and class component are –

* Function components are very minimal in nature. Its only requirement is to return a React element.

```
function Hello() { return '<div>Hello</div>' }
```

The same functionality can be done using ES6 class component with little extra coding.

class ExpenseEntryItem extends React.Component { render() { return (<div>Hello</div>); } }

* Class components supports state management out of the box whereas function components does not support state management. But, React provides a hook, useState() for the function components to maintain its state.

* Class component have a life cycle and access to each life cycle events through dedicated callback apis. Function component does not have life cycle. Again, React provides a hook, useEffect() for the function component to access different stages of the component.

<u>Creating a class component</u>

Let us create a new React component (in our expense-manager app), ExpenseEntryItem to showcase an expense entry item. Expense entry item consists of name, amount, date and category. The object representation of the expense entry item is –

{ 'name': 'Mango juice', 'amount': 30.00, 'spend_date': '2020-10-10' 'category': 'Food', }

Open expense-manager application in your favorite editor.

Next, create a file, ExpenseEntryItem.css under src/components folder to style our component.

Next, create a file, ExpenseEntryItem.js under src/components folder by extending React.Component.

import React from 'react'; import './ExpenseEntryItem.css'; class ExpenseEntryItem extends React.Component { }

Next, create a method render inside the ExpenseEntryItem class.

class ExpenseEntryItem extends React.Component { render() { } }

Next, create the user interface using JSX and return it from render method.

class ExpenseEntryItem extends React.Component { render() { return (<div> <div><b>Item:</b> <em>Mango Juice</em></div> <div><b>Amount:</b> <em>30.00</em></div> <div><b>Spend Date:</b> <em>2020-10-10</em></div> <div><b>Category:</b> <em>Food</em></div> </div>); } }

Next, specify the component as default export class.

import React from 'react'; import './ExpenseEntryItem.css'; class ExpenseEntryItem extends React.Component { render() { return (<div>

```
<div><b>Item:</b> <em>Mango Juice</em></div> <div><b>Amount:</b> <em>30.00</em></div> <div><b>Spend Date:</b> <em>2020-10-10</em></div> <div><b>Category:</b> <em>Food</em></div> </div> ); } } export default ExpenseEntryItem;
```

Now, we successfully created our first React component. Let us use our newly created component in index.js.

```
import React from ’react’; import ReactDOM from ’react-dom‘; import ExpenseEntryItem from ’./components/ExpenseEntryItem‘ ReactDOM.render( <React.StrictMode> <ExpenseEntryItem /> </React.StrictMode>, document.getElementById(’root‘) );
```

Example:

The same functionality can be done in a webpage using CDN as shown below –

```
<!DOCTYPE html> <html> <head> <meta charset="UTF-8" /> <title>React application :: ExpenseEntryItem component</title> </head> <body> <div id="react-app"></div> <script src="https://unpkg.com/react@17/umd/react.development.js" crossorigin></script> <script src="https://unpkg.com/react-dom@17/umd/react-dom.development.js" crossorigin></script> <script src="https://unpkg.com/@babel/standalone/babel.min.js"></script> <script type="text/babel"> class ExpenseEntryItem extends React.Component { render() { return ( <div> <div><b>Item:</b> <em>Mango Juice</em></div> <div><b>Amount:</b> <em>30.00</em></div> <div><b>Spend Date:</b> <em>2020-10-10</em></div> <div><b>Category:</b> <em>Food</em></div> </div> ); } } ReactDOM.render( <ExpenseEntryItem />, document.getElementById(’react-app’) ); </script> </body> </html>
```

Next, serve the application using npm command.

```
npm start
```

Output

Next, open the browser and enter http://localhost:3000 in the address bar and press enter.

Item: Mango Juice Amount: 30.00 Spend Date: 2020-10-10 Category: Food

Creating a function component

React component can also be created using plain JavaScript function but with limited features. Function based React component does not support state management and other advanced features. It can be used to quickly create a simple component.

The above ExpenseEntryItem can be rewritten in function as specified below –

function ExpenseEntryItem() { return (<div> <div><b>Item:</b> <em>Mango Juice</em></div> <div><b>Amount:</b> <em>30.00</em></div> <div><b>Spend Date:</b> <em>2020-10-10</em></div> <div><b>Category:</b> <em>Food</em></div> </div>); }

VII

ReactJS - Styling

React allows component to be styled using CSS class through className attribute. Since, the React JSX supports JavaScript expression, a lot of common CSS methodology can be used. Some of the top options are as follows –

CSS stylesheet – Normal CSS styles along with className

Inline styling – CSS styles as JavaScript objects along with camelCase properties.

CSS Modules – Locally scoped CSS styles.

Styled component– Component level styles.

Sass stylesheet– Supports Sass based CSS styles by converting the styles to normal css at build time.

Post processing stylesheet – Supports Post processing styles by converting the styles to normal css at build time.

*** CSS Stylesheet**

CSS stylesheet is usual, common and time-tested methodology. Simply create a CSS stylesheet for a component and enter all your styles for that particular component. Then, in the component, use className to refer the styles.

Let us style our ExpenseEntryItem component.

Open expense-manager application in your favorite editor.

Next, open ExpenseEntryItem.css file and add few styles.

div.itemStyle { color: brown; font-size: 14px; }

Next, open ExpenseEntryItem.js and add className to the main container.

```
import React from ’react‘; import ’./ExpenseEntryItem.css‘; class
ExpenseEntryItem extends React.Component { render() { return ( <div
className="itemStyle"> <div><b>Item:</b> <em>Mango Juice</em></div>
<div><b>Amount:</b> <em>30.00</em></div> <div><b>Spend Date:</b>
<em>2020-10-10</em></div> <div><b>Category:</b>
<em>Food</em></div> </div> ); } } export default ExpenseEntryItem;
```

Next, serve the application using npm command.

```
npm start
```

Next, open the browser and enter http://localhost:3000 in the address bar and press enter.

CSS stylesheet is easy to understand and use. But, when the project size increases, CSS styles will also increase and ultimately create lot of conflict in the class name. Moreover, loading the CSS file directly is only supported in Webpack bundler and it may not supported in other tools.

*** <u>Inline Styling</u>**

Inline Styling is one of the safest ways to style the React component. It declares all the styles as JavaScript objects using DOM based css properties and set it to the component through style attributes.

Let us add inline styling in our component.

Open expense-manager application in your favorite editor and modify ExpenseEntryItem.js file in the src folder. Declare a variable of type object and set the styles.

```
itemStyle = { color: ’brown‘, fontSize: ’14px‘ }
```

Here, fontSize represent the css property, font-size. All css properties can be used by representing it in camelCase format.

Next, set itemStyle style in the component using curly braces {} –

```
render() { return ( <div style={ this.itemStyle }> <div><b>Item:</b>
<em>Mango Juice</em></div> <div><b>Amount:</b>
<em>30.00</em></div> <div><b>Spend Date:</b>
<em>2020-10-10</em></div> <div><b>Category:</b>
<em>Food</em></div> </div> ); }
```

Also, style can be directly set inside the component –

```
render() { return ( <div style={ { color: ’brown‘, fontSize: ’14px‘ } }>
<div><b>Item:</b> <em>Mango Juice</em></div> <div><b>Amount:</b>
<em>30.00</em></div> <div><b>Spend Date:</b>
<em>2020-10-10</em></div> <div><b>Category:</b>
<em>Food</em></div> </div> ); }
```

Now, we have successfully used the inline styling in our application.

Next, serve the application using npm command.

npm start

Next, open the browser and enter http://localhost:3000 in the address bar and press enter.

*** <u>CSS Modules</u>**

Css Modules provides safest as well as easiest way to define the style. It uses normal css stylesheet with normal syntax. While importing the styles, CSS modules converts all the styles into locally scoped styles so that the name conflicts will not happen. Let us change our component to use CSS modules

Open expense-manager application in your favorite editor.

Next, create a new stylesheet, ExpenseEntryItem.module.css file under src/components folder and write regular css styles.

div.itemStyle { color: 'brown'; font-size: 14px; }

Here, file naming convention is very important. React toolchain will pre-process the css files ending with .module.css through CSS Module. Otherwise, it will be considered as a normal stylesheet.

Next, open ExpenseEntryItem.js file in the src/component folder and import the styles.

import styles from './ExpenseEntryItem.module.css'

Next, use the styles as JavaScript expression in the component.

<div className={styles.itemStyle}>

Now, we have successfully used the CSS modules in our application.

The final and complete code is –

import React from 'react'; import './ExpenseEntryItem.css'; import styles from './ExpenseEntryItem.module.css' class ExpenseEntryItem extends React.Component { render() { return (<div className={styles.itemStyle} > <div><b>Item:</b> <em>Mango Juice</em></div> <div><b>Amount:</b> <em>30.00</em></div> <div><b>Spend Date:</b> <em>2020-10-10</em></div> <div><b>Category:</b> <em>Food</em></div> </div>); } } export default ExpenseEntryItem;

Next, serve the application using npm command.

npm start

VIII
Props & State

Props: Props we will use for passing the information from one component to another component. Props are basically kind of global variable or object. We will learn about these in detail in this article. Passing and Accessing props. We can pass props to any component as we declare attributes for any HTML tag.

State: State is a built-in React object that is used to contain data or information about the component. A component's state can change over time; whenever it changes, the component re-renders.

State allows us to manage changing data in an application. It's defined as an object where we define key-value pairs specifying various data we want to track in the application. In React, all the code we write is defined inside a component.

```
class Greetings extends React.Component {
state = {
name: "World"
};
updateName() {
this.setState({ name: "Simplilearn" });
}
render() {
return(
<div>
{this.state.name}
</div>
)
```

}

}

Props example: Hello component with a name attribute can be accessed inside the component through this.props.name variable.

<Hello name="React" />

// value of name will be "Hello* const name = this.props.name

React properties supports attribute's value of different types. They are as follows,

* String
* Number
* Datetime
* Array
* List
* Objects

IX

ReactJS - Event management

Event management is one of the important features in a web application. It enables the user to interact with the application. React support all events available in a web application. React event handling is very similar to DOM events with little changes. Let us learn how to handle events in a React application in this chapter.

Let us see the step-by-step process of handling an event in a React component.

Define an event handler method to handle the given event.

log() { cosole.log("Event is fired"); }

React provides an alternative syntax using lambda function to define event handler. The lambda syntax is –

log = () => { cosole.log("Event is fired"); }

If you want to know the target of the event, then add an argument e in the handler method. React will send the event target details to the handler method.

log(e) { cosole.log("Event is fired"); console.log(e.target); }

The alternative lambda syntax is –

log = (e) => { cosole.log("Event is fired"); console.log(e.target); }

If you want to send extra details during an event, then add the extra details as initial argument and then add argument (e) for event target.

log(extra, e) { cosole.log("Event is fired"); console.log(e.target); console.log(extra); console.log(this); }

The alternative lambda syntax is as follows –

log = (extra, e) => { cosole.log("Event is fired"); console.log(e.target); console.log(extra); console.log(this); }

Bind the event handler method in the constructor of the component. This will ensure the availability of this in the event handler method.

constructor(props) { super(props); this.logContent = this.logContent.bind(this); }

If the event handler is defined in alternate lambda syntax, then the binding is not needed. this keyword will be automatically bound to the event handler method.

Set the event handler method for the specific event as specified below –

<div onClick={this.log}> ... </div>

To set extra arguments, bind the event handler method and then pass the extra information as second argument.

<div onClick={this.log.bind(this, extra)}> ... </div>

The alternate lambda syntax is as follows –

<div onClick={this.log(extra, e)}> ... </div>

X

ReactJS - Http Client Programming

Http client programming enables the application to connect and fetch data from http server through JavaScript. It reduces the data transfer between client and server as it fetches only the required data instead of the whole design and subsequently improves the network speed. It improves the user experience and becomes an indispensable feature of every modern web application.

Nowadays, lot of server side application exposes its functionality through REST API (functionality over HTTP protocol) and allows any client application to consume the functionality.

React does not provide it's own http programming api but it supports browser's built-in fetch() api as well as third party client library like axios to do client side programming.

Expense Rest Api Server

The prerequisite to do Http programming is the basic knowledge of Http protocol and REST API technique. Http programming involves two part, server and client. React provides support to create client side application. Express a popular web framework provides support to create server side application.

Let us first create a Expense Rest Api server using express framework and then access it from our ExpenseManager application using browser's built-in fetch api.

Open a command prompt and create a new folder, express-rest-api.

cd /go/to/workspace

mkdir apiserver

cd apiserver

Initialize a new node application using the below command –

npm init

The npm init will prompt and ask us to enter basic project details. Let us enter apiserver for project name and server.js for entry point. Leave other configuration with default option.

Next, install express, nedb & cors modules using below command –

npm install express nedb cors

express is used to create server side application.

nedb is a datastore used to store the expense data.

cors is a middleware for express framework to configure the client access details.

Next, let us create a file, data.csv and populate it with initial expense data for testing purposes. The structure of the file is that it contains one expense entry per line.

Pizza,80,2020-10-10,Food Grape Juice,30,2020-10-12,Food Cinema,210,2020-10-16,Entertainment Java Programming book,242,2020-10-15,Academic Mango Juice,35,2020-10-16,Food Dress,2000,2020-10-25,Cloth Tour,2555,2020-10-29,Entertainment Meals,300,2020-10-30,Food Mobile,3500,2020-11-02,Gadgets Exam Fees,1245,2020-11-04,Academic

Next, create a file expensedb.js and include code to load the initial expense data into the data store. The code checks the data store for initial data and load only if the data is not available in the store.

var store = require("nedb") var fs = require('fs'); var expenses = new store({ filename: "expense.db", autoload: true }) expenses.find({}, function (err, docs) { if (docs.length == 0) { loadExpenses(); } }) function loadExpenses() { readCsv("data.csv", function (data) { console.log(data); data.forEach(function (rec, idx) { item = {} item.name = rec[0]; item.amount = parseFloat(rec[1]); item.spend_date = new Date(rec[2]); item.category = rec[3]; expenses.insert(item, function (err, doc) { console.log('Inserted', doc.item_name, 'with ID', doc._id); }) }) }) } function readCsv(file, callback) { fs.readFile(file, 'utf-8', function (err, data) { if (err) throw err; var lines = data.split('\r\n'); var result = lines.map(function (line) { return line.split(','); }); callback(result); }); } module.exports = expenses

Next, create a file, server.js and include the actual code to list, add, update and delete the expense entries.

```
var express = require("express") var cors = require('cors') var expenseStore = require("./expensedb.js") var app = express() app.use(cors()); var bodyParser = require("body-parser"); app.use(bodyParser.urlencoded({ extended: false })); app.use(bodyParser.json()); var HTTP_PORT = 8000 app.listen(HTTP_PORT, () => { console.log("Server running on port %PORT%".replace("%PORT%", HTTP_PORT)) }); app.get("/", (req, res, next) => { res.json({ "message": "Ok" }) }); app.get("/api/expenses", (req, res, next) => { expenseStore.find({}, function (err, docs) { res.json(docs); }); }); app.get("/api/expense/:id", (req, res, next) => { var id = req.params.id; expenseStore.find({ _id: id }, function (err, docs) { res.json(docs); }) }); app.post("/api/expense/", (req, res, next) => { var errors = [] if (!req.body.item) { errors.push("No item specified"); } var data = { name: req.body.name, amount: req.body.amount, category: req.body.category, spend_date: req.body.spend_date, } expenseStore.insert(data, function (err, docs) { return res.json(docs); }); }) app.put("/api/expense/:id", (req, res, next) => { var id = req.params.id; var errors = [] if (!req.body.item) { errors.push("No item specified"); } var data = { _id: id, name: req.body.name, amount: req.body.amount, category: req.body.category, spend_date: req.body.spend_date, } expenseStore.update( { _id: id }, data, function (err, docs) { return res.json(data); }); }) app.delete("/api/expense/:id", (req, res, next) => { var id = req.params.id; expenseStore.remove({ _id: id }, function (err, numDeleted) { res.json({ "message": "deleted" }) }); }) app.use(function (req, res) { res.status(404); });
```

Now, it is time to run the application.

```
npm run start
```

Next, open a browser and enter http://localhost:8000/ in the address bar.

```
{ "message": "Ok" }
```

It confirms that our application is working fine.

Finally, change the url to http://localhost:8000/api/expense and press enter. The browser will show the initial expense entries in JSON format.

```
[ ... { "name": "Pizza", "amount": 80, "spend_date": "2020-10-10T00:00:00.000Z", "category": "Food", "_id": "5H8rK8lLGJPVZ3gD" }, ... ]
```

Let us use our newly created expense server in our Expense manager application through fetch() api in the upcoming section.

The fetch() api

Let us create a new application to showcase client side programming in React.

First, create a new react application, react-http-app using Create React App or Rollup bundler by following instruction in Creating a React application chapter.

Next, open the application in your favorite editor.

Next, create src folder under the root directory of the application.

Next, create components folder under src folder.

Next, create a file, ExpenseEntryItemList.css under src/components folder and include generic table styles.

html { font-family: sans-serif; } table { border-collapse: collapse; border: 2px solid rgb(200,200,200); letter-spacing: 1px; font-size: 0.8rem; } td, th { border: 1px solid rgb(190,190,190); padding: 10px 20px; } th { background-color: rgb(235,235,235); } td, th { text-align: left; } tr:nth-child(even) td { background-color: rgb(250,250,250); } tr:nth-child(odd) td { background-color: rgb(245,245,245); } caption { padding: 10px; } tr.highlight td { background-color: #a6a8bd; }

Next, create a file, ExpenseEntryItemList.js under src/components folder and start editing.

Next, import React library.

import React from ’react‘;

Next, create a class, ExpenseEntryItemList and call constructor with props.

class ExpenseEntryItemList extends React.Component { constructor(props) { super(props); } }

Next, initialize the state with empty list in the constructor.

this.state = { isLoaded: false, items: [] }

Next, create a method, setItems to format the items received from remote server and then set it into the state of the component.

setItems(remoteItems) { var items = []; remoteItems.forEach((item) => { let newItem = { id: item._id, name: item.name, amount: item.amount, spendDate: item.spend_date, category: item.category } items.push(newItem) }); this.setState({ isLoaded: true, items: items }); }

Next, add a method, fetchRemoteItems to fetch the items from the server.

fetchRemoteItems() { fetch("http://localhost:8000/api/expenses") .then(res => res.json()) .then((result) => { this.setItems(result); }, (error) => { this.setState({ isLoaded: false, error }); }) }

Here,

fetch api is used to fetch the item from the remote server.

setItems is used to format and store the items in the state.

Next, add a method, deleteRemoteItem to delete the item from the remote server.

```
deleteRemoteItem(id) { fetch('http://localhost:8000/api/expense/' + id, { method: 'DELETE' }) .then(res => res.json()) .then( () => { this.fetchRemoteItems() } ) }
```

Here,

fetch api is used to delete and fetch the item from the remote server.

setItems is again used to format and store the items in the state.

Next, call the componentDidMount life cycle api to load the items into the component during its mounting phase.

```
componentDidMount() { this.fetchRemoteItems(); }
```

Next, write an event handler to remove the item from the list.

```
handleDelete = (id, e) => { e.preventDefault(); console.log(id); this.deleteRemoteItem(id); }
```

Next, write the render method.

```
render() { let lists = []; if (this.state.isLoaded) { lists = this.state.items.map((item) => <tr key={item.id} onMouseEnter={this.handleMouseEnter} onMouseLeave={this.handleMouseLeave}> <td>{item.name}</td> <td>{item.amount}</td> <td>{new Date(item.spendDate).toDateString()}</td> <td>{item.category}</td> <td><a href="#" onClick={(e) => this.handleDelete(item.id, e)}>Remove</a></td> </tr> ); } return ( <div> <table onMouseOver={this.handleMouseOver}> <thead> <tr> <th>Item</th> <th>Amount</th> <th>Date</th> <th>Category</th> <th>Remove</th> </tr> </thead> <tbody> {lists} </tbody> </table> </div> ); }
```

Finally, export the component.

```
export default ExpenseEntryItemList;
```

Next, create a file, index.js under the src folder and use ExpenseEntryItemList component.

```
import React from 'react'; import ReactDOM from 'react-dom'; import ExpenseEntryItemList from './components/ExpenseEntryItemList'; ReactDOM.render( <React.StrictMode> <ExpenseEntryItemList /> </React.StrictMode>, document.getElementById('root') );
```

Finally, create a public folder under the root folder and create index.html file.

```
<!DOCTYPE html> <html lang="en"> <head> <meta charset="utf-8"> <title>React App</title> </head> <body> <div id="root"></div> <script type="text/JavaScript" src="./index.js"></script> </body> </html>
```

Next, open a new terminal window and start our server application.

```
cd /go/to/server/application npm start
```

Next, serve the client application using npm command.

```
npm start
```

XI
React.js - Redux

React redux is an advanced state management library for React. As we learned earlier, React only supports component level state management. In a big and complex application, large number of components are used. React recommends to move the state to the top level component and pass the state to the nested component using properties. It helps to some extent but it becomes complex when the components increases.

React redux chips in and helps to maintain state at the application level. React redux allows any component to access the state at any time. Also, it allows any component to change the state of the application at any time.

Let us learn about the how to write a React application using React redux in this chapter.

Concepts

React redux maintains the state of the application in a single place called Redux store. React component can get the latest state from the store as well as change the state at any time. Redux provides a simple process to get and set the current state of the application and involves below concepts.

Store – The central place to store the state of the application.

Actions – Action is an plain object with the type of the action to be done and the input (called payload) necessary to do the action. For example, action for adding an item in the store contains ADD_ITEM as type and an object with item's details as payload. The action can be represented as –

{ type: 'ADD_ITEM', payload: { name: '..', ... } }

Reducers – Reducers are pure functions used to create a new state based on the existing state and the current action. It returns the newly created state. For example, in add item scenario, it creates a new item list and merges the item from the state and new item and returns the newly created list.

Action creators – Action creator creates an action with proper action type and data necessary for the action and returns the action. For example, addItem action creator returns below object –

{ type: 'ADD_ITEM', payload: { name: '..', ... } }

Component – Component can connect to the store to get the current state and dispatch action to the store so that the store executes the action and updates it's current state.

The workflow of a typical redux store can be represented as shown below.

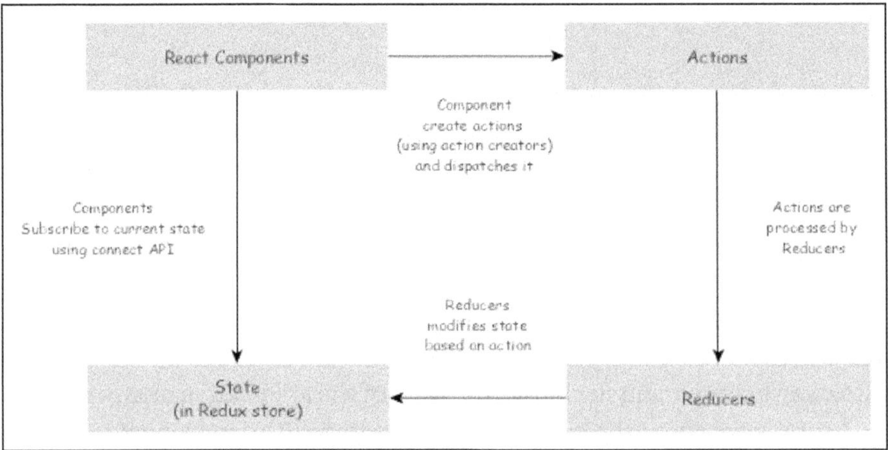

* React component subscribes to the store and get the latest state during initialization of the application.

* To change the state, React component creates necessary action and dispatches the action.

* Reducer creates a new state based on the action and returns it. Store updates itself with the new state.

* Once the state changes, store sends the updated state to all its subscribed component.

Redux API

Redux provides a single api, connect which will connect a components to the store and allows the component to get and set the state of the store.

The signature of the connect API is –

function connect(mapStateToProps?, mapDispatchToProps?, mergeProps?, options?)

All parameters are optional and it returns a HOC (higher order component). A higher order component is a function which wraps a component and returns a new component.

let hoc = connect(mapStateToProps, mapDispatchToProps) let connectedComponent = hoc(component)

Let us see the first two parameters which will be enough for most cases.

mapStateToProps – Accepts a function with below signature.

(state, ownProps?) => Object

Here, state refers current state of the store and Object refers the new props of the component. It gets called whenever the state of the store is updated.

(state) => { prop1: this.state.anyvalue }

mapDispatchToProps – Accepts a function with below signature.

Object | (dispatch, ownProps?) => Object

Here, **dispatch** refers the dispatch object used to dispatch action in the redux store and **Object** refers one or more dispatch functions as props of the component.

(dispatch) => { addDispatcher: (dispatch) => dispatch({ type: 'ADD_ITEM', payload: { } }), removeispatcher: (dispatch) => dispatch({ type: 'REMOVE_ITEM', payload: { } }), }

Provider Component

React Redux provides a Provider component and its sole purpose to make the Redux store available to its all nested components connected to store using connect API. The sample code is given below –

import React from 'react' import ReactDOM from 'react-dom' import { Provider } from 'react-redux' import { App } from './App' import createStore from './createReduxStore' const store = createStore() ReactDOM.render(<Provider store={store}> <App /> </Provider>, document.getElementById('root'))

Now, all the component inside the App component can get access to the Redux store by using connect API.

Working example

Let us recreate our expense manager application and uses the React redux concept to maintain the state of the application.

First, create a new react application, react-message-app using Create React App or Rollup bundler by following instruction in Creating a React application chapter.

Next, install Redux and React redux library.

npm install redux react-redux --save

Next, install uuid library to generate unique identifier for new expenses.

npm install uuid --save

Next, open the application in your favorite editor.

Next, create src folder under the root directory of the application.

Next, create actions folder under src folder.

Next, create a file, types.js under src/actions folder and start editing.

Next, add two action type, one for add expense and one for remove expense.

export const ADD_EXPENSE = 'ADD_EXPENSE'; export const DELETE_EXPENSE = 'DELETE_EXPENSE';

Next, create a file, index.js under src/actions folder to add action and start editing.

Next, import uuid to create unique identifier.

import { v4 as uuidv4 } from 'uuid';

Next, import action types.

import { ADD_EXPENSE, DELETE_EXPENSE } from './types';

Next, add a new function to return action type for adding an expense and export it.

export const addExpense = ({ name, amount, spendDate, category }) => ({ type: ADD_EXPENSE, payload: { id: uuidv4(), name, amount, spendDate, category } });

Here, the function expects expense object and return action type of ADD_EXPENSE along with a payload of expense information.

Next, add a new function to return action type for deleting an expense and export it.

export const deleteExpense = id => ({ type: DELETE_EXPENSE, payload: { id } });

Here, the function expects id of the expense item to be deleted and return action type of 'DELETE_EXPENSE' along with a payload of expense id.

The complete source code of the action is given below –

import { v4 as uuidv4 } from 'uuid'; import { ADD_EXPENSE, DELETE_EXPENSE } from './types'; export const addExpense = ({ name, amount, spendDate, category }) => ({ type: ADD_EXPENSE, payload: { id: uuidv4(), name, amount, spendDate, category } }); export const deleteExpense = id => ({ type: DELETE_EXPENSE, payload: { id } });

Next, create a new folder, reducers under src folder.

Next, create a file, index.js under src/reducers to write reducer function and start editing.

Next, import the action types.

import { ADD_EXPENSE, DELETE_EXPENSE } from '../actions/types';

Next, add a function, expensesReducer to do the actual feature of adding and updating expenses in the redux store.

export default function expensesReducer(state = [], action) { switch (action.type) { case ADD_EXPENSE: return [...state, action.payload]; case DELETE_EXPENSE: return state.filter(expense => expense.id !== action.payload.id); default: return state; } }

The complete source code of the reducer is given below –

import { ADD_EXPENSE, DELETE_EXPENSE } from '../actions/types'; export default function expensesReducer(state = [], action) { switch (action.type) { case ADD_EXPENSE: return [...state, action.payload]; case DELETE_EXPENSE: return state.filter(expense => expense.id !== action.payload.id); default: return state; } }

Here, the reducer checks the action type and execute the relevant code.

Next, create components folder under src folder.

Next, create a file, ExpenseEntryItemList.css under src/components folder and add generic style for the html tables.

html {font-family: sans-serif; } table { border-collapse: collapse; border: 2px solid rgb(200,200,200); letter-spacing: 1px; font-size: 0.8rem; } td, th { border: 1px solid rgb(190,190,190); padding: 10px 20px; } th { background-color: rgb(235,235,235); } td, th { text-align: left; } tr:nth-child(even) td {background-color: rgb(250,250,250); } tr:nth-child(odd) td { background-color: rgb(245,245,245); } caption { padding: 10px; } tr.highlight td { background-color: #a6a8bd; }

Next, create a file, ExpenseEntryItemList.js under src/components folder and start editing.

Next, import React and React redux library.

import React from 'react'; import { connect } from 'react-redux';

Next, import ExpenseEntryItemList.css file.

import './ExpenseEntryItemList.css';

Next, import action creators.

import { deleteExpense } from '../actions'; import { addExpense } from '../actions';

Next, create a class, ExpenseEntryItemList and call constructor with props.

class ExpenseEntryItemList extends React.Component { constructor(props) { super(props); } }

Next, create mapStateToProps function.

const mapStateToProps = state => { return { expenses: state }; };

Here, we copied the input state to expenses props of the component.

Next, create **mapDispatchToProps** function.

const mapDispatchToProps = dispatch => { return { onAddExpense: expense => { dispatch(addExpense(expense)); }, onDelete: id => { dispatch(deleteExpense(id)); } }; };

Here, we created two function, one to dispatch add expense **(addExpense)** function and another to dispatch delete expense **(deleteExpense)** function and mapped those function to props of the component.

Next, export the component using connect api.

export default connect(mapStateToProps, mapDispatchToProps)(ExpenseEntryItemList);

Now, the component gets three new properties given below –

* **expenses** – list of expense
* **onAddExpense** – function to dispatch addExpense function
* **onDelete** – function to dispatch deleteExpense function

Next, add few expense into the redux store in the constructor using onAddExpense property.

if (this.props.expenses.length == 0) { const items = [{ id: 1, name: "Pizza", amount: 80, spendDate: "2020-10-10", category: "Food" }, { id: 2, name: "Grape Juice", amount: 30, spendDate: "2020-10-12", category: "Food" }, { id: 3, name: "Cinema", amount: 210, spendDate: "2020-10-16", category: "Entertainment" }, { id: 4, name: "Java Programming book", amount: 242, spendDate: "2020-10-15", category: "Academic" }, { id: 5, name: "Mango Juice", amount: 35, spendDate: "2020-10-16", category: "Food" }, { id: 6, name: "Dress", amount: 2000, spendDate: "2020-10-25", category: "Cloth" }, { id: 7, name: "Tour", amount: 2555, spendDate: "2020-10-29", category: "Entertainment" }, { id: 8, name: "Meals", amount: 300, spendDate: "2020-10-30", category: "Food" }, { id: 9, name: "Mobile", amount: 3500, spendDate: "2020-11-02", category: "Gadgets" }, { id: 10, name: "Exam Fees", amount: 1245, spendDate: "2020-11-04", category: "Academic" }] items.forEach((item) => { this.props.onAddExpense({ name: item.name,

amount: item.amount, spendDate: item.spendDate, category: item.category }); }) }

Next, add an event handler to delete the expense item using expense id.

handleDelete = (id,e) => { e.preventDefault(); this.props.onDelete(id); }

Here, the event handler calls the onDelete dispatcher, which call deleteExpense along with the expense id.

Next, add a method to calculate the total amount of all expenses.

getTotal() { let total = 0; for (var i = 0; i < this.props.expenses.length; i++) { total += this.props.expenses[i].amount } return total; }

Next, add render() method and list the expense item in the tabular format.

render() { const lists = this.props.expenses.map((item) => <tr key={item.id}> <td>{item.name}</td> <td>{item.amount}</td> <td>{new Date(item.spendDate).toDateString()}</td> <td>{item.category}</td> <td><a href="#" onClick={(e) => this.handleDelete(item.id, e)}>Remove</a></td> </tr>); return (<div> <table><thead> <tr> <th>Item</th> <th>Amount</th> <th>Date</th> <th>Category</th> <th>Remove</th> </tr> </thead> <tbody> {lists} <tr> <td colSpan="1" style={{ textAlign: "right" }}>Total Amount</td> <td colSpan="4" style={{ textAlign: "left" }}> {this.getTotal()} </td> </tr> </tbody> </table></div>); }

Here, we set the event handler handleDelete to remove the expense from the store.

The complete source code of the ExpenseEntryItemList component is given below –

import React from ’react’; import { connect } from ’react-redux‘; import ’./ExpenseEntryItemList.css‘; import { deleteExpense } from ’../actions‘; import { addExpense } from ’../actions‘; class ExpenseEntryItemList extends React.Component { constructor(props) { super(props); if (this.props.expenses.length == 0){ const items = [{ id: 1, name: "Pizza", amount: 80, spendDate: "2020-10-10", category: "Food" }, { id: 2, name: "Grape Juice", amount: 30, spendDate: "2020-10-12", category: "Food" }, { id: 3, name: "Cinema", amount: 210, spendDate: "2020-10-16", category: "Entertainment" }, { id: 4, name: "Java Programming book", amount: 242, spendDate: "2020-10-15", category: "Academic" }, { id: 5, name: "Mango Juice", amount: 35, spendDate: "2020-10-16", category: "Food" }, { id: 6, name: "Dress", amount: 2000, spendDate: "2020-10-25", category: "Cloth" }, { id: 7, name: "Tour", amount: 2555,spendDate: "2020-10-29", category: "Entertainment" }, { id: 8, name: "Meals", amount: 300, spendDate:

```
"2020-10-30", category: "Food" }, { id: 9, name: "Mobile", amount: 3500, spendDate: "2020-11-02", category: "Gadgets" }, { id: 10, name: "Exam Fees", amount: 1245, spendDate: "2020-11-04", category: "Academic" } ] items.forEach((item) => { this.props.onAddExpense( { name: item.name, amount: item.amount, spendDate: item.spendDate, category: item.category } ); }) } } handleDelete = (id,e) => { e.preventDefault(); this.props.onDelete(id); } getTotal() { let total = 0; for (var i = 0; i < this.props.expenses.length; i++) { total += this.props.expenses[i].amount } return total; } render() { const lists = this.props.expenses.map((item) => <tr key={item.id}> <td>{item.name}</td> <td>{item.amount}</td> <td>{new Date(item.spendDate).toDateString()}</td> <td>{item.category}</td> <td><a href="#" onClick={(e) => this.handleDelete(item.id, e)}>Remove</a></td> </tr> ); return ( <div> <table> <thead> <tr> <th>Item</th><th>Amount</th> <th>Date</th> <th>Category</th> <th>Remove</th> </tr> </thead> <tbody> {lists} <tr> <td colSpan="1" style={{ textAlign: "right" }}>Total Amount</td> <td colSpan="4" style={{ textAlign: "left" }}> {this.getTotal()} </td> </tr> </tbody> </table> </div> ); }} const mapStateToProps = state => { return { expenses: state }; }; const mapDispatchToProps = dispatch => { return { onAddExpense: expense => { dispatch(addExpense(expense)); }, onDelete: id => { dispatch(deleteExpense(id)); } }; }; export default connect( mapStateToProps, mapDispatchToProps )(ExpenseEntryItemList);
```

Next, create a file, App.js under the src/components folder and use ExpenseEntryItemList component.

```
import React, { Component } from 'react'; import ExpenseEntryItemList from './ExpenseEntryItemList'; class App extends Component { render() { return ( <div> <ExpenseEntryItemList /> </div> ); } } export default App;
```

Next, create a file, index.js under src folder.

```
import React from 'react'; import ReactDOM from 'react-dom'; import { createStore } from 'redux'; import { Provider } from 'react-redux'; import rootReducer from './reducers'; import App from './components/App'; const store = createStore(rootReducer); ReactDOM.render( <Provider store={store}> <App /> </Provider>, document.getElementById('root') );
```

Here,

Create a store using createStore by attaching the our reducer.

Used Provider component from React redux library and set the store as props, which enables all the nested component to connect to store using connect api.

Finally, create a public folder under the root folder and create index.html file.

```
<!DOCTYPE html> <html lang="en"> <head> <meta charset="utf-8"> <title>React Containment App</title> </head> <body> <div id="root"></div> <script type="text/JavaScript" src="./index.js"></script> </body> </html>
```

Next, serve the application using npm command.

```
npm start
```

www.ingramcontent.com/pod-product-compliance
Ingram Content Group UK Ltd.
Pitfield, Milton Keynes, MK11 3LW, UK
UKHW021925190726
13853UKWH00002B/856